The Police Station

Aaron Carr

AV² WORLD LANGUAGES

Go to **av2books.com**, and enter this book's unique code.

BOOK CODE

AVJ49385

This is my neighborhood.

The police station is in my neighborhood.

Toggle between your **ten books** in **ten languages.**

Click **READ** to **hear** full audio.

Easily move through highly visual pages.

AV² WORLD LANGUAGES   The Police Station   BACK READ NEXT   Change Language

English Spanish French Arabic Korean
Russian Mandarin German Hindi Tagalog

Published by AV² by Weigl
350 5th Avenue, 59th Floor New York, NY 10118
Website: www.av2books.com

Library of Congress Control Number: 2019938126

ISBN 978-1-4896-6985-8 (hardcover)
ISBN 978-1-4896-6986-5 (multi-user eBook)

Printed in Guangzhou, China
1 2 3 4 5 6 7 8 9 0 23 22 21 20 19

042019
122118

Project Coordinators: Megan Cuthbert and Heather Kissock Design: Mandy Christiansen

Weigl acknowledges Getty Images as the primary image supplier for this title.
Page 10 Image: pio3 / Shutterstock.com. Page 12 Main Image: justasc / Shutterstock.com..

The Police Station

CONTENTS

2 AV² Book Code
4 My Neighborhood
6 What Is a Police Station?
8 Meet the Police Officer
10 Spot the Police Officer
12 Police Station Tools
14 Getting Around
16 Helping Out
18 Visit the Police Station
20 In the Neighborhood
22 Police Station Quiz
24 Key Words

This is my neighborhood.

The police station is in my neighborhood.

People call the police station if they are in danger.

They can also go to the police station if they need to talk to a police officer.

I see police officers in my neighborhood.

They make sure people follow the law.

Police officers make sure my neighborhood is safe.

I can spot them easily because they wear a uniform.

Police officers drive special cars.

Police cars have flashing lights and loud sirens.

Some police officers ride bicycles or horses in my neighborhood.

Sometimes people stop and ask the police questions.

If I am lost or hurt I can go to the police for help.

Police help the people in my neighborhood when they do not feel safe.

17

I can visit the police station with my class from school.

The police officer lets me and my friends sit in a police car.

Police officers take part in neighborhood events.

They visit my school and teach me and my friends about safety.

21

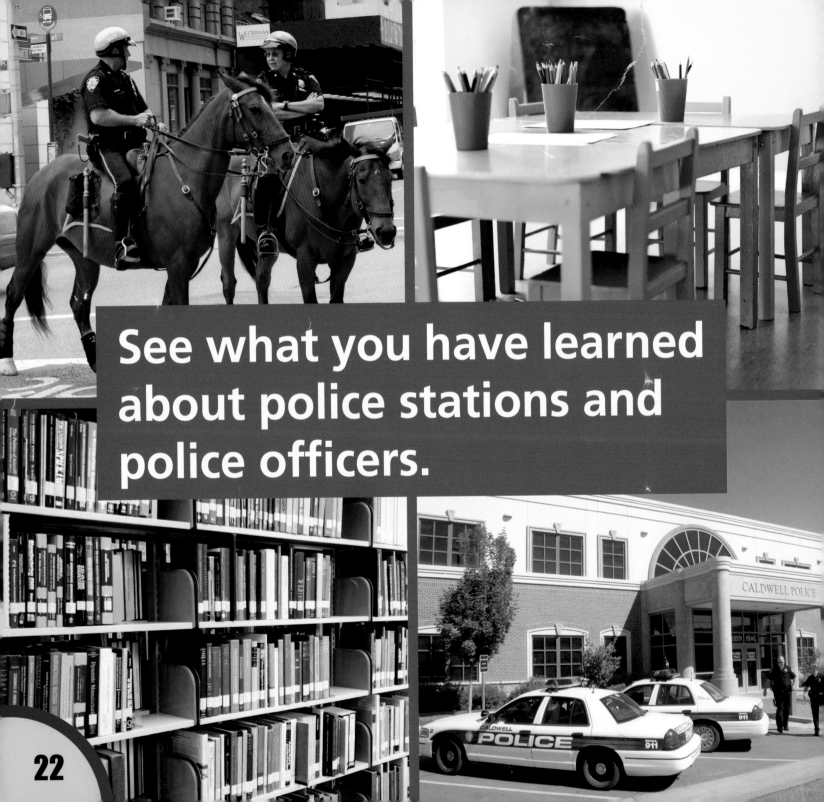

See what you have learned about police stations and police officers.

Which of these pictures does not show a police station?

23

KEY WORDS

Research has shown that as much as 65 percent of all written material published in English is made up of 300 words. These 300 words cannot be taught using pictures or learned by sounding them out. They must be recognized by sight. This book contains 44 common sight words to help young readers improve their reading fluency and comprehension. This book also teaches young readers several important content words, such as proper nouns. These words are paired with pictures to aid in learning and improve understanding.

Page	Sight Words First Appearance
4	is, my, this
5	in, the
6	are, call, if, people, they
7	a, also, can, go, need, talk, to
8	I, see
9	make
11	because, them
12	cars
13	and, have, lights
14	or, some
15	sometimes, stop
16	am, for, help
17	do, not, when
18	from, school, with
19	lets, me
20	part, take
21	about

Page	Content Words First Appearance
4	neighborhood
5	police station
6	danger
7	police officer
9	law
11	uniform
13	sirens
14	bicycles, horses
15	questions
18	class
19	friends
20	events
21	safety